The Voyage of MAE JEMISON

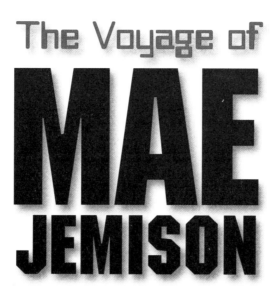

Susan Canizares • Samantha Berger

Scholastic Inc.
New York • Toronto • London • Auckland • Sydney

Acknowledgments

Literacy Specialist: Linda Cornwell

Social Studies Consultant: Barbara Schubert, Ph.D.

Design: Silver Editions

Photo Research: Silver Editions

Endnotes: Elizabeth Scholl

Endnote Illustrations: Anthony Carnabucia

Photographs: Cover portrait: NASA; cover background: Sygma;
pp. 1–2, 5–7, 10, 11: NASA; p. 3: Nasa/Gamma Liaison; p. 4, 12: Sygma;
pp. 8, 9: NASA/Ressmeyer/Corbis.

Library of Congress Cataloging-in-Publication Data
Canizares, Susan 1960-
The voyage of Mae Jemison / Susan Canizares, Samantha Berger.
p. cm. -- (Social studies emergent readers)
Summary: Simple text and photographs of Mae Jemison and other astronauts introduce some aspects of living and working in space.
ISBN 0-439-04579-7 (pbk.: alk. paper)
1. Astronautics--Juvenile literature. 2. Jemison, Mae, 1956- --
Journeys--Juvenile literature. 3.Space flight--Juvenile literature.
[1. Space flight. 2. Jemison, Mae, 1956- .]
I. Berger, Samantha. II. Title. III. Series.
TL793.C36 1999
629.45'0092--dc21   Copyright © 1999 by Scholastic Inc.   98-53308
Illustrations copyright © 1999 by Scholastic Inc.
All rights reserved. Published by Scholastic Inc.
Printed in the U.S.A.

8   9   10   08   03

Mae and her team are going into space.

First they must train.

Then they must practice.

Now they can say good-bye.

3 - 2 - 1 - Blast off!

In space, everything is different.

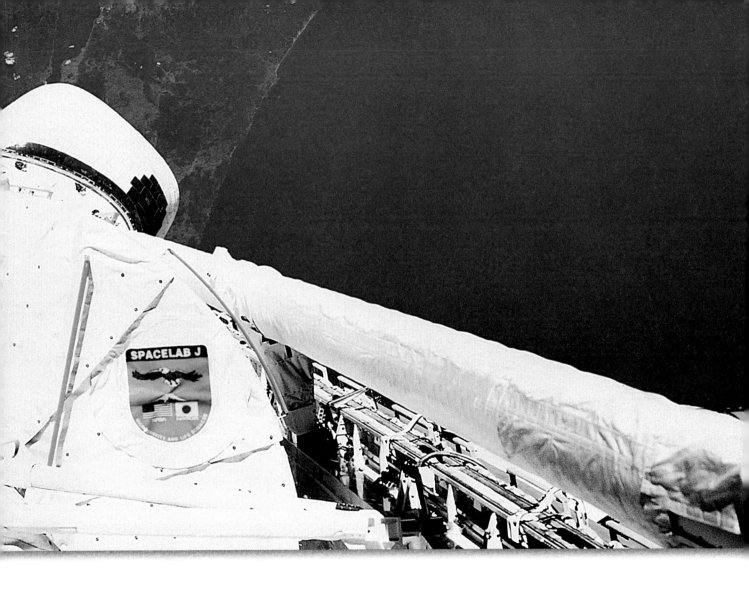

Drinking is different.

Eating is different.

Walking is different.

Working is different.

Having fun is different, too!

The Voyage of **MAE JEMISON**

Mae Jemison was born in Alabama on October 17, 1956, and moved to Chicago, Illinois, when she was three years old. Chicago is where Mae grew up. Mae was the youngest of the three children in her family.

By the time she was in kindergarten, Mae had many different interests. She wanted to be not only a scientist but also an archaeologist, astronomer, architect, fashion designer, writer, and dancer! She spent many hours at the library, reading all the books she could find about dinosaurs, science, and space. Mae also enjoyed working on science projects for school. When she watched *Star Trek* or saw astronauts and space flights on television and in the news, Mae knew someday she would go into space.

Mae graduated from high school as an honor student and then continued her studies at Stanford University in California. Her major areas of study were chemical engineering and African and Afro-American studies.

After receiving her science degree at Stanford University, Mae attended Cornell University Medical College in New York. As part of her training to become a doctor, she traveled to Cuba, Kenya, and Thailand, where she helped provide medical care for people in need. In 1981, when Mae was almost 25 years old, she received her doctor of medicine degree and began working as a physician in Los Angeles, California.

Wishing to continue helping people in other parts of the world, as she had done during medical school, Mae worked for the Peace Corps, an organization whose goal is to improve conditions for people in developing countries. Mae was sent to West Africa. Two years later, Mae returned to her medical practice in Los Angeles. She was now working on another plan. Mae had decided to

try to become an astronaut. She applied to the National Aeronautics and Space Administration (NASA). Mae Jemison was one of just 15 people chosen from the 2,000 who had applied.

Mae moved to Houston, Texas, where she trained at the Johnson Space Center. She studied survival techniques and space shuttle equipment and operations. Astronauts have lots of other jobs while training and waiting to go into space—Mae worked at the Kennedy Space Center helping to get the space shuttle ready for launch. She tested the computer programs that control the shuttle and also helped to design experiments. At the end of a year, Mae had become a mission specialist astronaut. She had to wait several years, but she finally was able to go into space.

Mae was chosen to be a member of the crew of the space shuttle *Endeavor*. On September 12, 1992, at 10:23 A.M., the *Endeavor* lifted off on its journey. It was an eight-day mission. Dr. Mae Jemison was the first African-American woman in space. She worked on several experiments during the shuttle mission, including a new way of controlling space sickness. Many astronauts feel dizzy and nauseated when they go into space. Mae also worked on a frog embryology experiment. She began raising tadpoles in space and then let them continue to grow to adulthood back on earth. The frogs developed normally, the same way they would have if they had been on the earth the whole time!

After her space mission, Mae received many awards and honors. She resigned from the astronaut corps in 1993 in order to form her own company, which works toward improving conditions in poor countries as well as working with advancing technologies in developing countries. Currently she is a professor of environmental studies at Dartmouth College. She also spends time traveling and giving speeches, encouraging young people to follow their dreams—as she did.